THE SPANISH CONQUISTADORS CONQUER THE AZTECS

HISTORY 4TH GRADE

Children's History Books

BABY PROFESSOR
EDUCATION KIDS

Speedy Publishing LLC

40 E. Main St. #1156

Newark, DE 19711

www.speedypublishing.com

Copyright 2017

In the 1520s, a tiny force of adventurers from Europe came to what is now Mexico and conquered the Aztec Empire of six million people. How did this happen? Read on and see!

THE AZTECS AND THE NEWCOMERS

The Aztec Empire, centered in what is now Mexico, dominated the region between about 1350 and 1520. It was an alliance of three powerful city-states that absorbed many other cultures in what is now Mexico.

MOCTEZUMA

The Aztecs were originally a people from the north of Mexico. They moved south around 1100, and after great difficulty over many years established themselves among the tribes and city-states of central Mexico. They made allies and began a rise to dominance over the whole region.

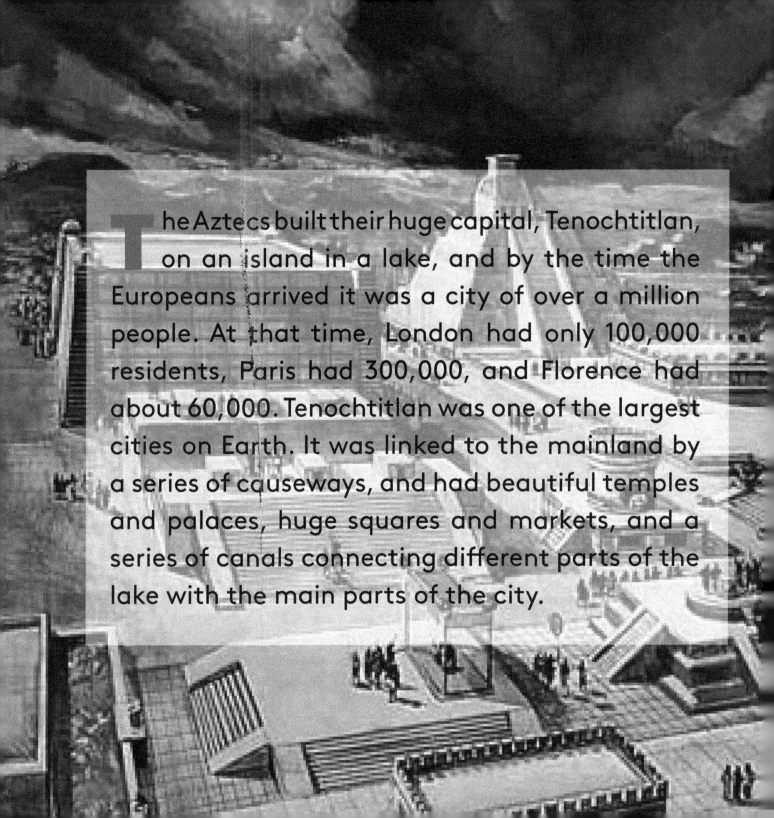

The Aztecs built their huge capital, Tenochtitlan, on an island in a lake, and by the time the Europeans arrived it was a city of over a million people. At that time, London had only 100,000 residents, Paris had 300,000, and Florence had about 60,000. Tenochtitlan was one of the largest cities on Earth. It was linked to the mainland by a series of causeways, and had beautiful temples and palaces, huge squares and markets, and a series of canals connecting different parts of the lake with the main parts of the city.

CHRISTOPHER COLUMBUS

Europeans were excited by the "discovery" of the Americas by Christopher Columbus in 1492. (Read about him in the Baby Professor book Who was Christopher Columbus?) They imagined fantastic cities of gold and huge mines of silver and jewels. Spain, France, and England, in particular, sent out explorers and adventurers to see what they could find and claim for their country.

ARRIVAL

Spain already had bases in the Caribbean islands. There was a report of immense riches in what is now Mexico. In 1521 the governor of Cuba sent Hernán Cortés, with a few hundred men, to explore the area and trade with the native people, but not to invade or conquer anything. Cortés had never led an army, but he had dreams of glory.

HERNÁN CORTÉS

SIGNS AND WONDERS

Aztec sources say that, in this time, there were many signs of some amazing thing that would happen. They included:

- A column of fire blazed through one night, in 1517.

- A fire destroyed the temple of Huitzilopochtli, one of the Aztec's main gods.

- A lightning strike destroyed a temple of another god, Xiutecuhtli.

- Three comets appeared, streaking across the daytime sky at the same time.

- A lake near the capital started bubbling or boiling.

MONTEZUMA INSTRUCTS THE
PEOPLE TO LAY DOWN THEIR ARMS

As well, the emperor, Montezuma (sometimes written "Moctezuma"), had frightening dreams and visions. As the emperor was a high priest as well as a political leader, people took his visions seriously.

The Aztecs believed their hundreds of gods were present and active in their everyday life, and saw great significance in such events. This prepared them to wonder if the arriving Spaniards were not invaders, but messengers from the gods—or perhaps gods themselves!

THE SPANISH ADVANCE

After the Spanish landed, they learned about the Aztec Empire. They found that many parts of the empire resented the Aztecs and would do almost anything to be free of them.

AZTEC EMPIRE

Cortés was able to gather allies for his small force of 500 men. Sometimes he won them over with promises of liberation; sometimes he defeated armies in battle and then demanded

STORMING OF THE TEOCALLI BY CORTEZ
AND HIS TROOPS

that that tribe join him against the Aztecs. To "convince" a defeated city, Cortés would often have all its leaders killed.

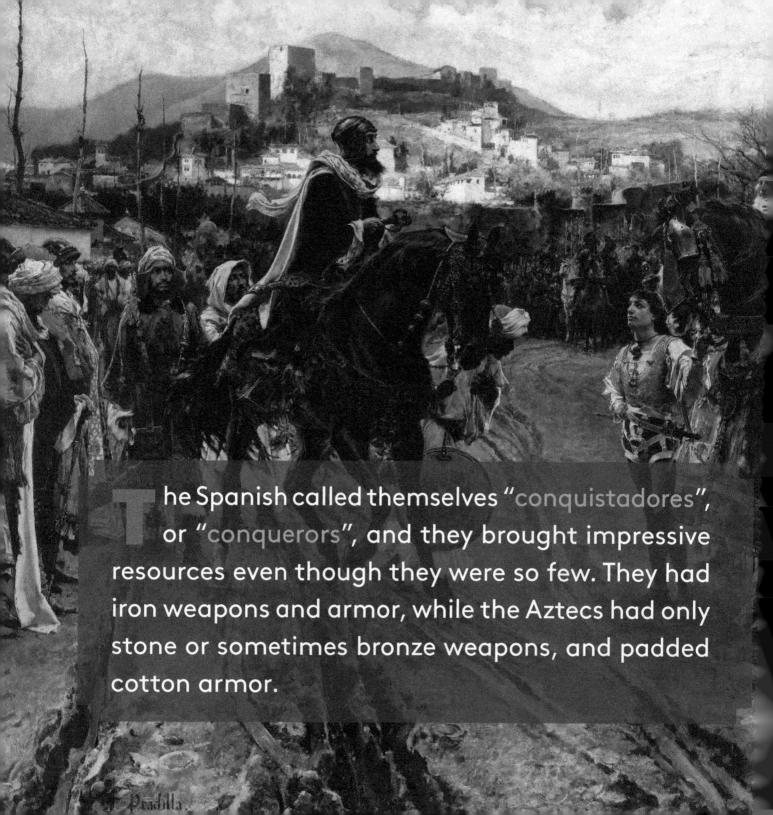

The Spanish called themselves "conquistadores", or "conquerors", and they brought impressive resources even though they were so few. They had iron weapons and armor, while the Aztecs had only stone or sometimes bronze weapons, and padded cotton armor.

The conquistadores had cannon and muskets, which absolutely astonished the Aztecs as they had never seen such a thing before. Even more astonishing, the Spaniards rode on horses. There were no horses in North America at this

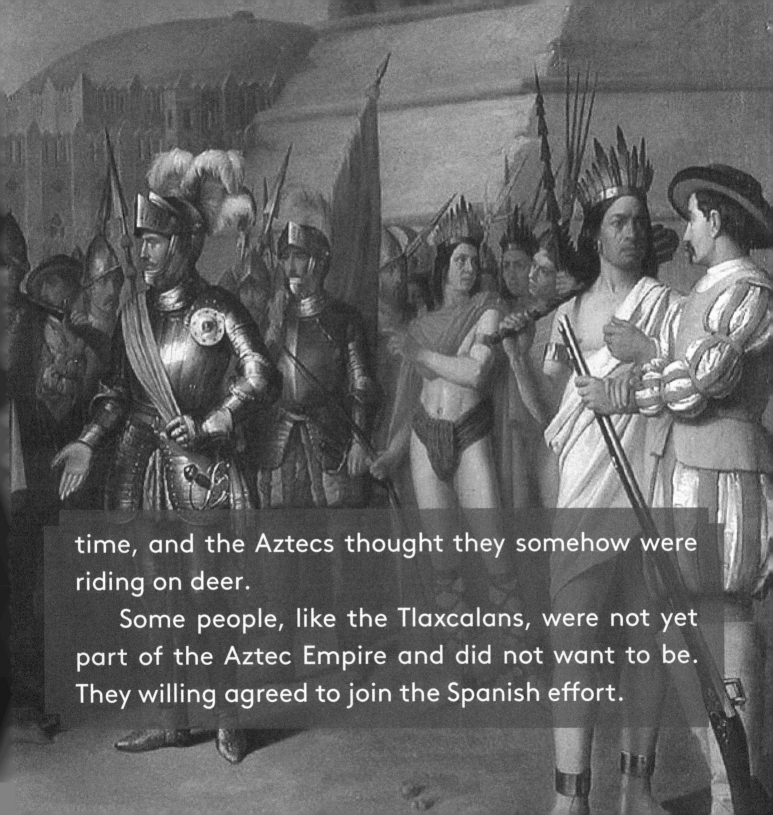

time, and the Aztecs thought they somehow were riding on deer.

Some people, like the Tlaxcalans, were not yet part of the Aztec Empire and did not want to be. They willing agreed to join the Spanish effort.

ARRIVAL AT TENOCHTITLAN

It took eight months for Cortés and his growing army to move inland to Tenochtitlan, where they arrived in November, 1519. Montezuma invited them into the city, although he could have overwhelmed them with the huge Aztec army.

The conquistadors enter
Tenochtitlan

Shortly after, Cortés took advantage of a battle in which some of his soldiers died to arrest Montezuma and hold him captive.

Six months later Cortés heard of more Spaniards arriving from Cuba—coming to arrest him! The governor was not pleased with Cortés conquering instead of trading. Cortés took part of his army to deal with this threat, leaving Pedro de Alvarado in charge of the city.

SLAUGHTER

With Cortés away, Alvorado gave permission for a great Aztec feast to honor the chief god, Huitzilopochtli. This was the main celebration in a calendar of feasts and sacrifices essential to Aztec culture. Read more about their gods in the Baby Professor book The Aztecs' Many Gods.

AZTEC MARKET AT
TLATELOLCO, MEXICO

AZTECS RISE AGAINST THE CONQUISTADORS

Hundreds of leading Aztecs gathered in a main square, without their weapons, to feast, dance, and honor Huitzilopochtli. While the festival was going on, Alvorado had his troops surround the square. Then they attacked, killing almost all the unarmed Aztecs.

The city erupted in violence, with Aztecs attacking the Spaniards from all sides. Their weight of numbers was greater than the Spaniards' superior weapons, and the Spaniards had to retreat into a fortified area.

Cortez Conquering Mexico City

LA NOCHE TRISTE

When Cortés had dealt with the new group of Spaniards (most of them joined his army!) and returned to Tenochtitlan, he decided his forces would have to retreat. They tried have Montezuma speak to the people to calm things down, but the Aztecs were outraged with their emperor, who had let the Spaniards into the city. He died during the fighting, possibly struck down by an Aztec weapon.

As the Spaniards retreated out of the city along the causeways one night in June, 1520, they were attacked from all sides. In Spanish histories of the Conquest, this is called "La noche triste", or "The Sorrowful Night." Over 700 Spaniards died, and as many as three thousand of their allies, before they were able to fight clear and move back to the coast to regroup and for the wounded to heal.

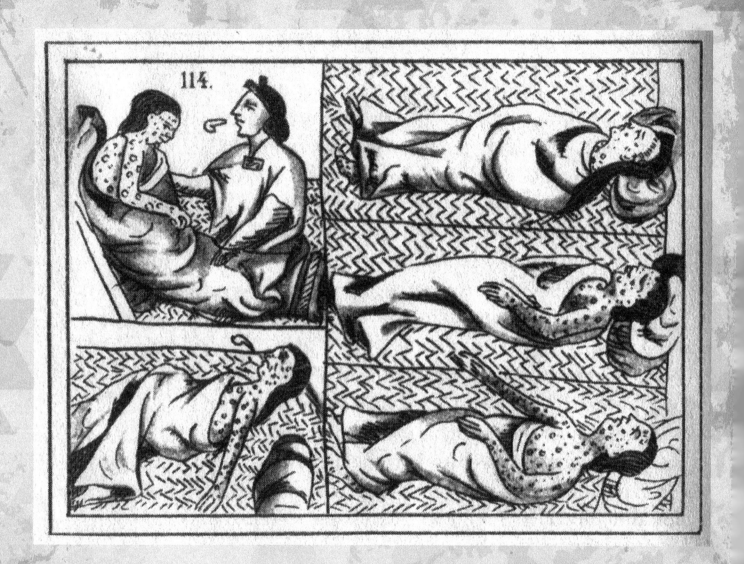

SMALLPOX OUTBREAK

A SECRET ALLY

The Spaniards did not know it, but they had a secret weapon in their fight: germs. Some of the conquistadores carried the disease smallpox, having survived it themselves. Smallpox was unknown until then in the Americas, and the Aztec people had little resistance to it. Millions of Aztecs died, including much of the army. Cuitlahuac, who became emperor after the death of Montezuma, himself died of smallpox eighty days later.

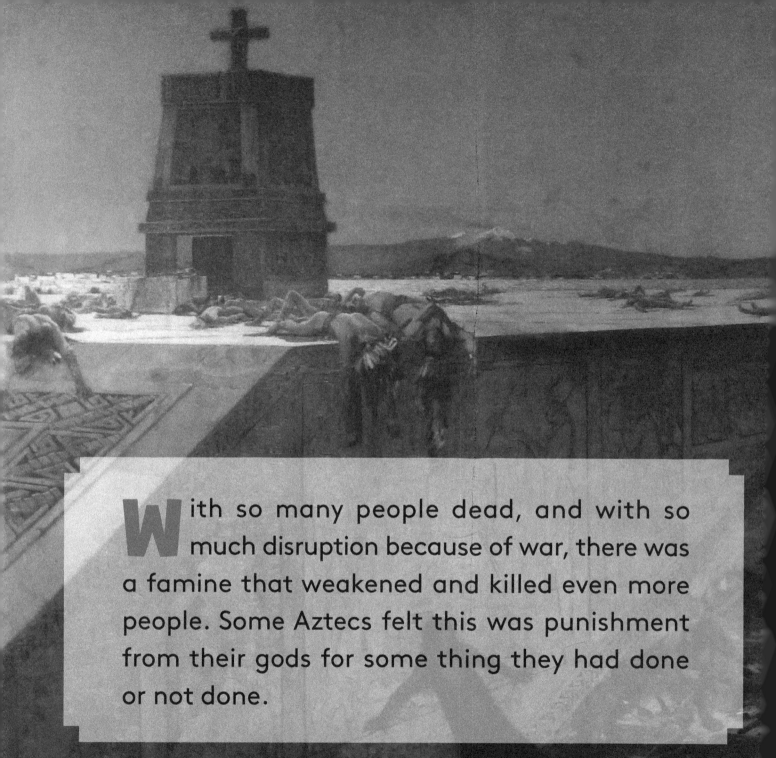

With so many people dead, and with so much disruption because of war, there was a famine that weakened and killed even more people. Some Aztecs felt this was punishment from their gods for some thing they had done or not done.

When Cortés returned after five months, with his conquistadores and his allies, in August, 1521, they found the capital, Tenochtitlan, devastated. Nevertheless, the Aztecs, under Emperor Cuauhtemoc, who had followed his cousin Cuitlahuac, resisted the invaders for a siege and series of battles lasting 75 days.

CONQUISTADORS EXHORT
THEIR SUPPORTERS

All the Aztec allies had gone over to the Spanish side, including the Texcoco, a people who had helped found the empire with the Aztecs. Half of the population of the city was dead and there were little food supplies. Yet still the Aztecs fought on.

The Spaniards blocked the canals so canoes could not bring supplies. They blocked the causeways to make it harder for the Aztec fighters to come out of the city. They poisoned the sources of drinking water.

When the city finally surrendered, some Spaniards wrote accounts of what they saw. They wrote that they had never seen such suffering, and they did not understand how the Aztecs had held out so long.

The final Aztec surrender was on August 13, 1521. The Spaniards captured the emperor, Cuauhtemoc, and put him to death. He was the last Aztec emperor, and his death symbolized the end of a once-great empire and the arrival of a new power in the land.

Monumento of Cuauhtemoc

Aztec Ruins

AFTER THE CONQUEST

After the city surrendered, the conquistadores destroyed it. They broke down temples and palaces, set houses on fire, and blocked the causeways so people could not easily travel to and from the city.

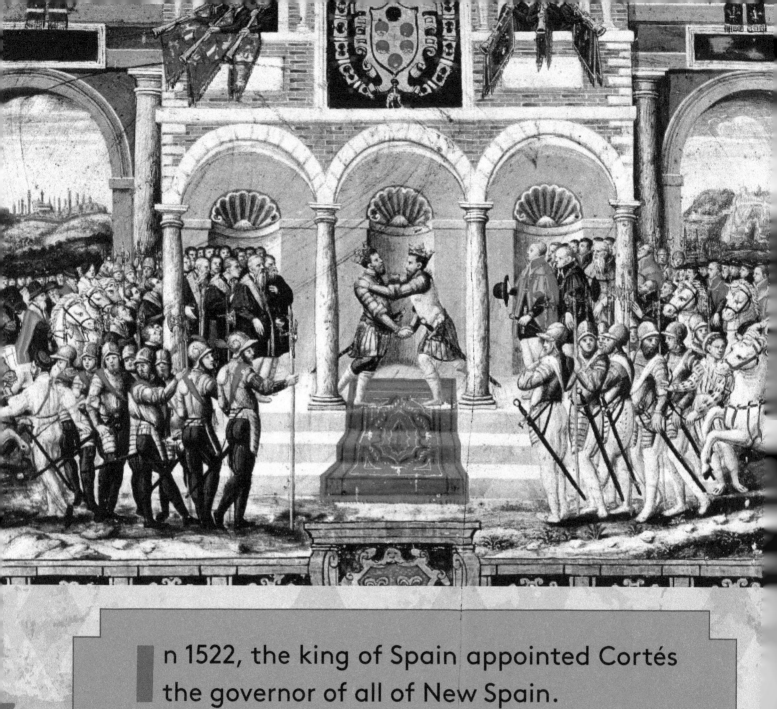

n 1522, the king of Spain appointed Cortés the governor of all of New Spain.

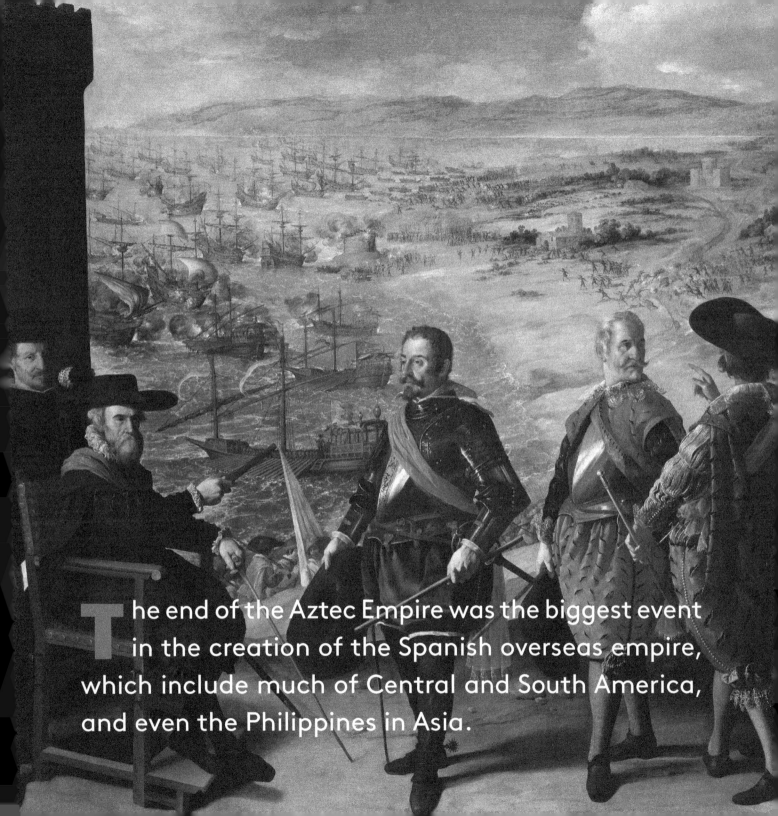

The end of the Aztec Empire was the biggest event in the creation of the Spanish overseas empire, which include much of Central and South America, and even the Philippines in Asia.

THE AZTEC WORLD

Although the Aztecs were defeated, they were not a primitive people. Read the Baby Professor book Aztec Technology and Art to learn more about what they had developed, and what they lacked, when the invaders arrived.

TENOCHTITLAN

Also, read about the Aztecs' neighbors to the north in the Baby Professor book Getting to Know the Great Native American Tribes.

CPSIA information can be obtained
at www.ICGtesting.com
Printed in the USA
BVHW061245220722
642605BV00004B/348

9 781541 912106